EXPERT

Golf Rules
Quick Reference

A practical guide for use on the course. Stroke Play & Match Play.

Water-repellent

Golf Guide & Logbook

For before and after a round

- Golf course guide
- Ratings portal
- Personal logbook

- Apple
- Recommended by
- Relief finder
- Step by step videos
- 200+ images

Virtual Referee

Find the right solution with 3 clicks

Videos

Relief Finder

Match Play

Stroke Play

iGolfrules
Version 2016-2019

EXPERT GOLF
get there

Free app

Logbook

Golf guide

EXPERT GOLF
get there

EXPERT GOLF
get there

Summary of the most important rules changes valid from 2016

Moved by the player—put it back, 1 penalty stroke

Moved by the wind—play from new position, no penalty

Ball moved when addressing it (Rule 18-2)

Previously, if the ball moved after the player had addressed it, it was assumed that the player had caused the ball to move. He incurred 1 penalty stroke. An exception to this were cases in which it was obvious that the player was not responsible for the ball moving.

Now, it is no longer automatically assumed that the player is at fault and the sole determining factor is who or what caused the ball to move. If it was the player he must put the ball back and he incurs 1 penalty stroke. If, for example, it was the wind or if the ball moved on its own it must be played from its new position and no penalty is incurred.

Distance measuring devices
(Rule 14-3 and Appendix IV)

Since 2006, distance measuring devices can be permitted by Local Rule. However, they are only allowed to measure the distance and the player is not permitted to use any prohibited functions (e.g. measuring the slope). Previously, it was deemed a breach of the rules if a function such as this was installed on the device, irrespective of whether the player had actually used it.

Now, the sole determining factor is whether the player uses a prohibited function.

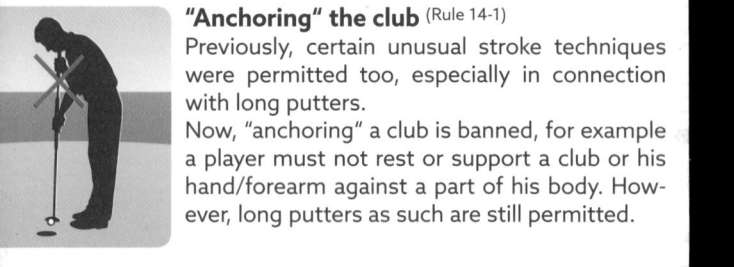

Prohibited devices (Rule 14-3)

Previously, a player who used an artificial device or unusual equipment was immediately disqualified.

Now, the penalty is applied in stages—with the first infringement the player incurs 2 penalty strokes (in match play, he loses the hole) and he is only disqualified if he breaches the rule again.

"Anchoring" the club (Rule 14-1)

Previously, certain unusual stroke techniques were permitted too, especially in connection with long putters.

Now, "anchoring" a club is banned, for example a player must not rest or support a club or his hand/forearm against a part of his body. However, long putters as such are still permitted.

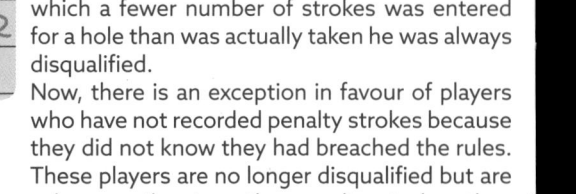

Submission of a score card with fewer strokes than taken (Rule 6-6)

Previously, if a player handed in a score card on which a fewer number of strokes was entered for a hole than was actually taken he was always disqualified.

Now, there is an exception in favour of players who have not recorded penalty strokes because they did not know they had breached the rules. These players are no longer disqualified but are subsequently given the penalty strokes they failed to record, plus an additional penalty of 2 strokes.

How to use this guide

Step 1
The overview on the last page shows whether you are entitled to relief.

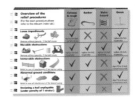

Step 2
Refer to the index tab which corresponds to the position of your ball or to the place where the incident occurred.

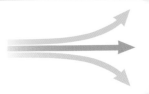

Step 3
Use the headings and illustrations to find the right solution for your particular situation.

(Generally speaking, the topics are dealt with in chronological order within a chapter, i.e. in the same order as they would occur in the course of a game. Firstly, problems in connection with finding the ball, its lie, the practice swing, addressing the ball, etc. are dealt with. These issues are followed by relief procedures and finally, incidents which can occur when a stroke is played are explained.)

☛ The rule number can be found in brackets after each heading, thus making it easy to consult the official rule book as required.

☛ Always observe any Local Rules and Conditions of Competition.

☛ Please abide by the etiquette—serious breaches can result in disqualification.

Basics and dropping

Stroke play and match play (R2/3)

In general, the same rules apply to match play as they do to stroke play. However, whereas during stroke play the basic penalty for a breach of the rules is 2 penalty strokes, in match play the player immediately loses the hole.

Differing match play rules are printed in grey and italics in this book.

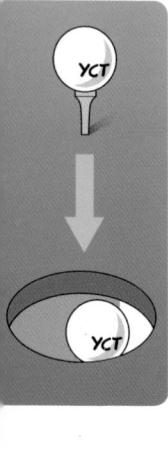

Holing out and conceding (R2/3/32)

In principle, the ball that is teed off with must be played into the hole (holed out), otherwise the player could be disqualified. A hole can only be given up without holing out in certain forms of play (e.g. Stableford).

In principle, the ball can only be changed between holes, otherwise 2 penalty strokes are incurred (unless, of course, the ball is lost or is in a water hazard etc.).

MATCH PLAY: A hole can be given up without holing out. Furthermore, the player can concede that his opponent has holed out with his next stroke. Conceded shots can neither be refused nor withdrawn. If the player who has been given the hole plays it to the end anyway the result is not affected.

Caddie (R6)

Please remember that as a player you are responsible for everything your caddie does. If your caddie breaches a rule you, as the player, will be penalised for it.

Playing the ball as it lies (R13)

The basic principle of the game of golf says if a rule does not allow anything else, you should

- not touch the ball in between the tee and the green,
- play the ball as it lies (or if its lie has been changed it should be played as it lay when it came to rest),

- play the course as you find it.

If you play the ball as it lies, it is practically impossible to do anything wrong unless the ball is *out of bounds*, on the *wrong green* or in an area where playing is *not permitted as stated in the Local Rules* (e.g. ground under repair, environmentally-sensitive area).

Play two balls (only in stroke play)

When in doubt about the rules (R2/3)

If you are not sure how to proceed and cannot decide between two courses of action you can play two balls. Inform your fellow-competitors which of the two balls is to count in the event that *both* options conform to the rules and then play both balls until you have holed out. Note down both scores—upon completion of the round you *must* clarify the matter with the Committee *before* signing and handing in your score card.

MATCH PLAY: Playing two balls is not an option—the players have to find a solution themselves. If you do not agree with your opponent's actions you can make a "claim" immediately, stating your reasons, and have the matter clarified by the Committee later.

Dropping and re-dropping (Def./R20/21)

Dropping means to let a ball drop from shoulder height with the arm stretched horizontally. The place where you drop is not to be nearer to the hole. You are always permitted to clean a ball which is to be dropped.

The ball must be dropped a second time, without an additional penalty, if it rolls into one of the following positions.

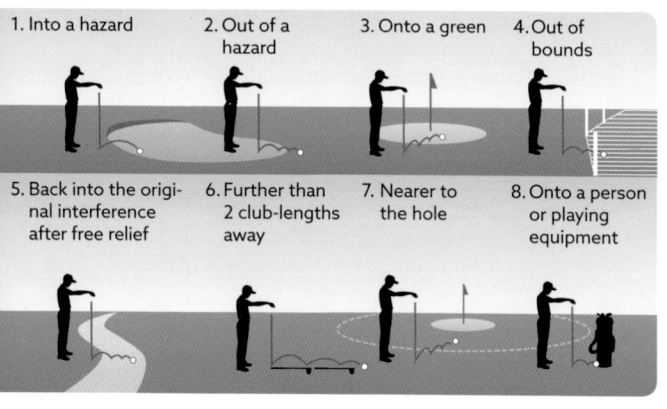

1. Into a hazard
2. Out of a hazard
3. Onto a green
4. Out of bounds
5. Back into the original interference after free relief
6. Further than 2 club-lengths away
7. Nearer to the hole
8. Onto a person or playing equipment

If one of the situations from 1-7 occurs when the ball is dropped for a second time, the ball must be placed on the spot where it hit the ground when it was re-dropped. If the ball does not stay in this position, it must be placed at the nearest point where it does not roll away.

*If situation 8 occurs the ball must be re-dropped until it no longer hits a person or playing equipment.

Drop twice then place the ball*

👉 Summary: Drop twice then place the ball—unless a person or playing equipment are hit.

Incorrect drop (R20)

If you have dropped the ball on the wrong spot or in the wrong manner but have *not yet played* the ball, you are allowed to pick the ball up without penalty and drop it correctly.

If you have *already played* the ball the following penalties apply.

- **Dropped on the wrong spot**
  2 penalty strokes for playing from the wrong spot (disqualification possible if the wrong spot resulted in a significant improvement or an advantage in terms of distance).

- **Dropped in an incorrect manner**
  1 penalty stroke for dropping incorrectly (e.g. not dropped from shoulder height or with the arm not stretched out).

Suspension of play/ thunder storm (R6)

If play has been suspended by means of a warning signal (e.g. blasts of a horn) you *have to stop playing*. Mark your ball, pick it up and place it on the same spot again later. You are also allowed to complete a hole which has already been started.

☞ Please remember that you do *not* have to wait for play to be suspended officially if you believe the situation to be dangerous.

If players discontinue their round without a valid reason, e.g. just because of rain, they could be disqualified.

No practicing on the course (R7)

No practicing on the competition course is permitted on the day of a tournament, either before or during a round (or between rounds if a tournament takes place over several rounds).

MATCH PLAY: Permitted before the round.

On the tee

Late arrival (R6)

If a player arrives late within 5 minutes of his tee-off time he will usually incur 2 penalty strokes. If he is more than 5 minutes late, he is usually disqualified.

Maximum of 14 clubs (R4)

A maximum of 14 clubs is allowed. If you have brought too many, you must, in principle, remove the extra clubs from your bag *before beginning* the round.

If you only notice that you have too many clubs *after starting the round*, you must immediately declare them to be out of play, and you are then no longer permitted to use them (disqualification).

You will incur 2 penalty strokes for each hole on which you had too many clubs, to a maximum of 4 penalty strokes per round.

👉 You are not permitted to borrow a club from another player on the course in order to play a stroke with it.

The honor/ order of play (R10)

On the first tee, the order of play is taken from the order of the draw (list of tee times). On the following tees, the person who had the best result at the previous hole has the honor to tee off first.

MATCH PLAY: The player who won the previous hole has the honor.

1. 2.

Unintentional —no penalty

Playing in the wrong order (R10)

If a player tees off out of turn, the stroke counts anyway, and you do not incur a penalty. However, if the players have *agreed* upon the wrong order so that one of them gains a *tactical advantage*, they will be punished with disqualification.

MATCH PLAY: Without penalty, however the opponent may immediately require the player to cancel his stroke and replay it in the correct order.

Teeing ground (Def./R11)

The teeing ground extends from the tee-markers to 2 club-lengths behind the markers. The *ball* must be teed up within this area; however, the player can take up his stance outside it. A ball is outside the teeing ground when the entire ball is outside it.

Playing from outside the teeing ground (R11)

If a player tees off from outside the teeing ground, the stroke does not count and he incurs 2 penalty strokes. The player has to rectify the mistake by teeing off again within the teeing ground (3rd stroke).

☞ If the mistake is not rectified the player will be disqualified.

MATCH PLAY: Without penalty, however the opponent may immediately require the player to cancel and replay his stroke.

Playing from the wrong teeing ground (R11)

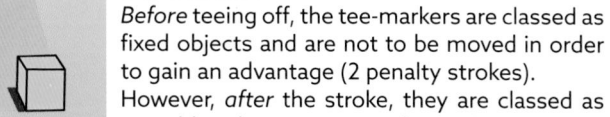

If a player plays from the wrong teeing ground, even if this is further back and he would not gain an advantage from it, the same rule applies as when playing from outside the teeing ground (see previous page).

Tee-markers (R11)

Before teeing off, the tee-markers are classed as fixed objects and are not to be moved in order to gain an advantage (2 penalty strokes).

However, *after* the stroke, they are classed as movable obstructions and can be removed without penalty.

Relief (R11/13/23/24)

On the tee, uneven ground can be smoothed out, and you can even pull up grass. All loose objects which disturb you in any way, whether they are natural or artificial (except for the tee-markers), can be removed without penalty.

Ball falls off tee (R11)

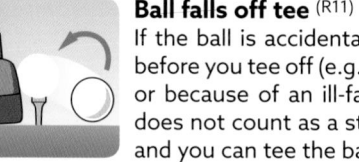

If the ball is accidentally knocked from the tee before you tee off (e.g. when addressing the ball or because of an ill-fated practice swing), this does not count as a stroke. There is no penalty and you can tee the ball up again.

Air shot (Def./R11)

Every stroke counts, even if you accidentally missed the ball.

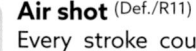 After an air shot, the ball is in play, and it can no longer be touched.

Advice and line of play (R8)

You are allowed to discuss distances, the position of hazards or out of bounds margins, the pin position, the rules and other general facts. If you cannot see the green from the tee, you are allowed to ask someone to indicate its position. However, you are not allowed to *ask* for or *give* advice ("Which club did you take?", "Which club should I play?", "Take a 7 iron.", etc.), otherwise 2 penalty strokes will be incurred.
A player who is given unsolicited advice does not receive any penalty strokes.

Provisional/ lost ball (R27)

If you suspect that you will not be able to find your ball or that it has landed out of bounds, you should play a provisional ball. Announce that it is "provisional", tee it up, and then play it until you reach the approximate position where you believe the original ball to be. (Then proceed as described under the index tab "Out/ prov. ball.")

Play a provisional ball

👉 If you do not explicitly announce that the second ball is "provisional", it becomes the new ball in play under penalty of 1 stroke.

No provisional ball

👉 If your ball has landed in a *water hazard*, you do *not* have the option of playing a provisional ball.

Chipping and putting to kill time (R7)

You are allowed to putt and chip on the teeing ground while you are waiting to tee off.

Through the green (fairway, rough, etc.)

- Fairway
- Semi-rough
- Rough
- Other teeing grounds
- Other greens

Definition (Def.)

The term "through the green" includes every fairway and all areas of semi-rough, rough and fringe, plus all other teeing grounds as well as greens *which do not belong to the hole*. If you are on any other part of the course (tee, bunker, water hazard, out of bounds, green) please select the relevant index tab.

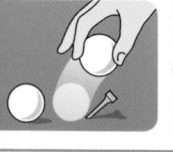

Playing in the wrong order (R10)

It is always the turn of the player whose ball is furthest away from the hole. If a player makes a stroke out of turn the stroke counts anyway and a penalty is not incurred. (Exception: Agreeing on the wrong order of play for tactical reasons leads to disqualification.)

MATCH PLAY: Without penalty, however the opponent may immediately require the player to cancel his stroke and replay it in the correct order.

Balls close to each other (R22)

If two balls are so close together that they obstruct each other, one ball can be marked, picked up and put back again after the other one has been played.

Take a drop, no penalty

Embedded ball (R25)

If your ball has become embedded into the ground upon landing on a *closely-mown* area (fairway, fringe, green but not semi-rough or rough)*, you are allowed to pick it up, clean it and let it drop right next to the original spot.

☞ *Bear the Local Rules in mind—they often grant relief everywhere through the green by way of exception.*

Looking for a ball (Def./R27)

You have a maximum of 5 minutes to find your ball. After this time has run out, the ball is classed as lost, and you have to take a drop on the spot where the last stroke was played from (tee up on the teeing ground), incurring 1 penalty stroke.

⏱ 5 min.

Identifying the ball (R12)

If you cannot tell whether the ball found is yours, you are allowed to mark it and pick it up for identification. However, before doing so, you must inform a fellow-player of this and give him the opportunity to observe the procedure; otherwise, you will incur 1 penalty stroke. If necessary, you may clean the ball but only to the extent needed for identification. The ball is then to be put back on exactly the same spot.

Ball moved during a search (R18)

If *you* unintentionally move your ball during a search, you must put it back, and you will receive 1 penalty stroke (without penalty if you are searching in abnormal ground conditions or in obstructions). If you do not put it back, you will be playing from the wrong spot, and you will incur 2 penalty strokes.

If a *fellow-player* moves your ball it must also be put back but this does not incur a penalty.

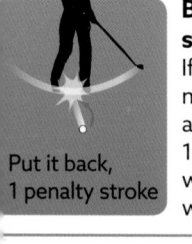

Put it back,
1 penalty stroke

Ball moved when taking a practice swing (R18)

If you take a practice swing and accidentally move your ball in doing so this does *not* count as a stroke, and you must put the ball back with 1 penalty stroke. If you do not put it back, you will incur 2 penalty strokes for playing from the wrong spot.

Put it back,
1 penalty stroke

Ball moved when addressing it (R18)

If, by grounding your club, you cause the ball to move you must put it back under penalty of 1 stroke. If you do not put it back, you will incur 2 penalty strokes for playing from the wrong spot.

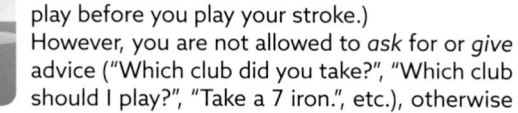

Advice and line of play (R8)

You are allowed to discuss distances, the position of hazards or out of bounds margins, the pin position, the rules and other general facts. If you cannot see the flag, you are allowed to ask someone to indicate the line of play. (If a marking has been positioned on the line of play or a person is marking it for you, the marking must be removed or the person must leave the line of play before you play your stroke.)

However, you are not allowed to *ask* for or *give* advice ("Which club did you take?", "Which club should I play?", "Take a 7 iron.", etc.), otherwise 2 penalty strokes will be incurred.

A player who is given unsolicited advice does not receive any penalty strokes.

Do not break anything off or bend anything out of the way (R13)

You have to accept the lie as you find it. You are not permitted to *move, bend or break off* anything growing or fixed *before* making a stroke in order to improve the lie of the ball, the area of stance or swing or the line of play (2 penalty strokes).

You will also be given 2 penalty strokes if you bend or break off anything while making a *practice swing* if this will be of advantage to your shot.

Loose impediments (R23)

Leaves, twigs, stones, grass cuttings or other *natural* objects can be removed without penalty. If the ball moves as a result—put it back, 1 penalty stroke.

☞ Note: Sand and loose soil can only be removed on the green, not through the green (2 penalty strokes).

Movable obstructions (R24)

Bottles, cans, signs, stakes (yellow, red, blue) or other *artificial* objects can be removed without penalty. If the ball moves as a result—put it back, without penalty.

Even if the ball is lying *in* or *on* the obstruction, the obstruction can be removed. The ball is then to be *dropped* at its original position.

☞ Note: Removing *out of bounds posts* is *never* permitted (2 penalty strokes).

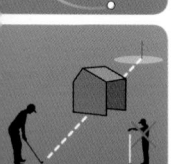

Immovable obstructions ^(R24)

Roads and paths with an *artificial surface* or other *fixed, artificial* objects entitle you to *free* relief if they interfere with the *ball's lie*, your *stance* or your *swing* (not if they only interfere with the *line of play*).

To take relief, locate the nearest point where you can take your stance and swing without interference from the obstruction and drop the ball within 1 club-length.

In the illustration below, point A is the nearest point. There is no interference in the case of point B either, but this spot is further away from the ball's original position.

Take a drop, no penalty

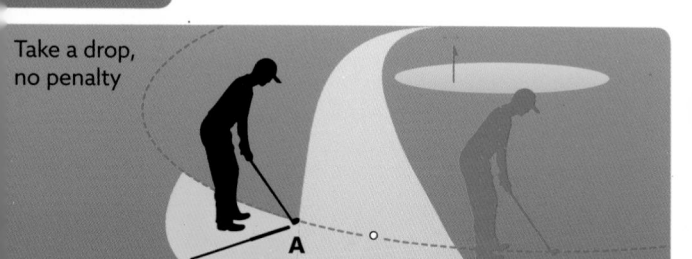

🖙 Please note—it is possible that the nearest point will be in a bush, in the rough or on a slope. It may then be advisable to play the ball as it lies.

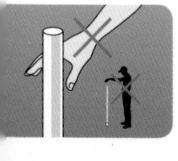

🖙 Relief is not given from objects which mark out of bounds. Furthermore, Local Rules can declare certain objects as being an integral part of the course. Relief is not given if this is the case.

Abnormal ground conditions (R25)

This includes ground under repair (usually marked in blue or mentioned in the Local Rules), casual water (visible puddles) and excavation tracks caused by burrowing animals (primarily mole hills and mouse and rabbit holes). It also includes grass or other material piled up to be removed as well as holes made by greenkeepers. If you accidentally move the ball when searching for it in abnormal ground conditions put it back, without penalty.

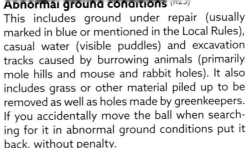

If your ball is lying within one of the above-mentioned areas, or if you would have to take your stance within one, you are given free relief. Find the nearest point where your ball is no longer within this area and where you do not have to take your stance within it and drop the ball within 1 club-length.

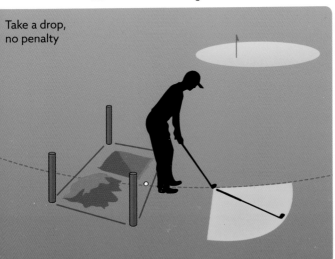

Take a drop, no penalty

Take a drop,
no penalty

Ball lost in abnormal ground conditions (R25)

If you cannot find your ball but you are sure that it could only be lost in abnormal ground conditions, you are also given free relief. Proceed in exactly the same way as described on the previous page, but the starting point is not the ball, it is the spot where your ball last crossed the margin of the abnormal ground conditions.

Take a drop,
no penalty

Wrong green (R25)

If your ball lands on the wrong green (including a practice green), you are not allowed to play it from there. You *have* to take free relief. Go to the nearest edge of the green, as always not nearer to the hole, and drop your ball within 1 club-length. This will usually be on the fringe. You are allowed to take your stance on the green to play a ball which is not on the green.

Bad luck—play
the ball as it
lies

Divots, tractor ruts, bald patches, etc. (R13)

If your ball has a bad lie which is not explicitly dealt with by the rules, then there is nothing you can do about it. You have to play the ball as it lies unless you declare it unplayable (with 1 penalty stroke, see below).

Unplayable Ball (R28)

If a ball has an extremely bad lie it is advisable to declare it unplayable. The player is free to choose whether to do this or not, and it does not need to be agreed by the marker. You then have three possibilities to drop the ball, each incurring 1 penalty stroke.

1. Take a drop within 2 club-lengths, 1 penalty stroke.
2. Take a drop on the backwards extension of the line from the hole to the ball, 1 penalty stroke.
3. Take a drop on the site of the last stroke (tee up on the tee), 1 penalty stroke.

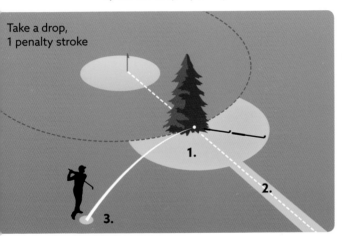

Take a drop,
1 penalty stroke

1.

2.

3.

👉 If, when dropped, the ball rolls back to the unplayable position or has a bad lie for any other reason, there is nothing you can do about it. It either has to be played as it lies, or it can be declared unplayable once again, incurring *another* penalty stroke.

Wrong ball (R15)

If you have played the wrong ball, this stroke does not count but you will incur 2 penalty strokes. You have to go back and play the correct ball (put the wrong ball back).

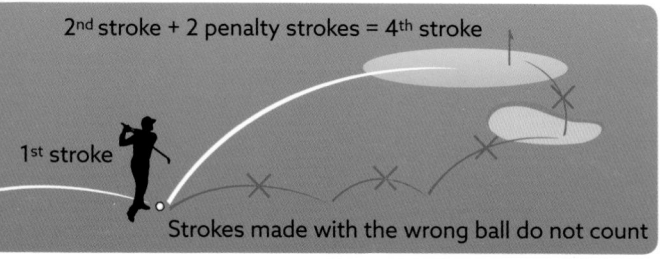

2nd stroke + 2 penalty strokes = 4th stroke

1st stroke

Strokes made with the wrong ball do not count

If you cannot find the correct ball, you have to return to the place where you last played the correct ball from and drop another ball with 1 additional penalty stroke (tee up on the teeing ground).

If you hole out with the wrong ball and do not rectify your mistake, you will be disqualified.

Ball hits an outside agency (R19)

If your ball hits an electricity pole, a tree, a spectator, an animal, another ball or any other outside agency, you do not incur a penalty, and the ball has to be played as it lies.

MATCH PLAY: If your ball hits the opponent or his equipment no penalty is incurred. You can continue to play the ball as it lies or you can choose to cancel the stroke and replay it (drop the ball).

"Rub of the green"—play the ball as it lies

Ball hits the player or his equipment (R19)

If you yourself or your equipment (golf bag, electric cart, etc.) are hit by your ball, 1 penalty stroke will be incurred, and the ball has to be played as it lies.

1 penalty stroke

Ball at rest moved by an outside agency (R18)

If your ball *at rest* is moved by an outside agency (spectator, animal, fellow-competitor, other ball, etc.), you have to put your ball back without penalty. If your ball has been picked up and taken away, you are permitted to place *another* ball on the spot where the ball was, without penalty.

Put it back, no penalty

MATCH PLAY: If your ball is moved by the opponent during a search, there is no penalty. If a search is not involved, the opponent incurs 1 penalty stroke. The ball has to be put back.

Lost ball (R27)

If you cannot find your ball after looking for it for 5 minutes, or if you cannot unequivocally identify it as your own (for example, you find two identical balls or you cannot remember the brand and number of the ball you were playing with), it is classed as lost. Take a drop on the site of the last stroke (tee up on the teeing ground), 1 penalty stroke.

Striking the ball more than once (R14)

If you accidentally strike the ball more than once when playing a shot, you have to add 1 penalty stroke to it.

In the bunker

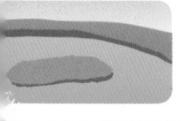

Margin (Def.)

The ball is classed as being in a bunker if it touches the sand within it. Areas of grass in the bunker are not part of the bunker.

Identifying the ball (R12)

If you cannot tell whether the ball found is yours, you are allowed to mark it and pick it up for identification. However, before doing so, you must inform a fellow-player of this and give him the opportunity to observe the procedure; otherwise, you will incur 1 penalty stroke. The ball is then to be put back on exactly the same spot. In doing so, the original lie has to be reproduced as accurately as possible (i.e. rake the sand, bury the ball if appropriate, etc.).

Ball disappeared in the sand (R12)

If you cannot find your ball although you clearly saw it land in a bunker it has probably sunk into the sand. You are permitted to probe the sand and rake it in order to locate your ball. If the ball moves as a result—put it back, without penalty, and recreate the original lie. You have a maximum of 5 minutes to find your ball.

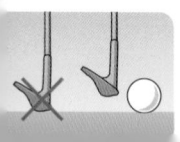

Do not touch or test the sand (R13)

The condition of the bunker is not to be tested before playing a stroke, i.e. do not touch the sand or rake it, do not make any practice

sand on your back swing; otherwise, you will incur 2 penalty strokes.

However, you can put the rake or a club down in the sand. Furthermore it is permitted to smooth out prints if the purpose is solely course maintenance, if the prints are not on the line of play and the player does not gain an advantage for his next stroke in doing so.

Balls close to each other (R20/22)

If two balls are so close together that they obstruct each other, one ball can be marked, picked up and put back afterwards. In doing so, the original lie must be reproduced as accurately as possible (i.e. rake the sand, bury the ball if appropriate, etc.).

Advice and line of play (R8)

You are allowed to ask about distances as well as the position of hazards or out of bounds margins. If you cannot see the flag from the bunker, you are allowed to ask someone to indicate the line of play. However, *questions* or *advice* on the choice of club or how to play a shot would incur 2 penalty strokes.

Loose impediments (R23)

Twigs, leaves, stones* or other *natural* objects *must not* be touched or removed before playing a stroke from a bunker (2 penalty strokes).

☞ *Bear the Local Rules in mind—they often stipulate that stones can be removed without penalty by way of exception.

No penalty

Movable obstructions (R24)

Artificial objects can be removed without penalty. If the sand is touched when doing so no penalty is incurred. If the ball moves as a result, put it back without penalty.

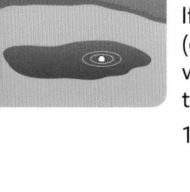

Abnormal ground conditions (R25)

If the ball is lying in abnormal ground conditions (e.g. a puddle, ground under repair) or if you would have to take your stance within it you can take relief.

1. Without penalty, take a drop *in the bunker*, at the nearest point where the interference is eliminated as much as possible, within 1 club-length.
2. With 1 penalty stroke, take a drop *outside of the bunker*, on the backwards extension of the line from the hole to the ball.

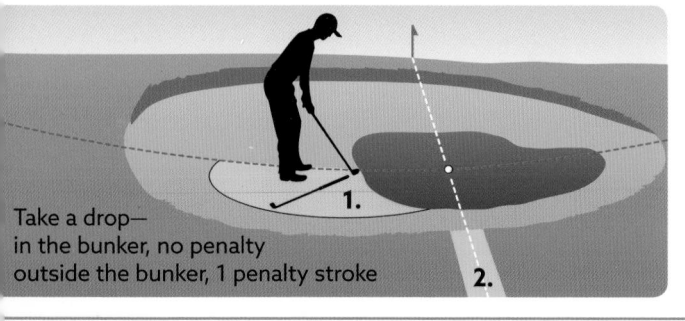

Take a drop—
in the bunker, no penalty
outside the bunker, 1 penalty stroke

1.

2.

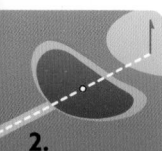

2.

Bunker completely flooded (R25)

If the bunker is completely under water, the player has effectively no other choice but to proceed in accordance with the 2nd option (see above). He then has to accept 1 penalty stroke.

If your ball has a bad lie which is not explicitly dealt with by the rules, then there is nothing you can do about it. You have to play the ball as it lies unless you declare it unplayable (with 1 penalty stroke, see below).

Unplayable ball (R28)

If a ball in a bunker is declared unplayable, the player has three options to drop a ball, each linked to 1 penalty stroke.

1. Take a drop *in the bunker* within 2 club-lengths, 1 penalty stroke.
2. Take a drop *in the bunker* on the backwards extension of the line from the hole to the ball, 1 penalty stroke.
3. Take a drop on the site of the last stroke (tee up on the teeing ground), 1 penalty stroke.

Bu

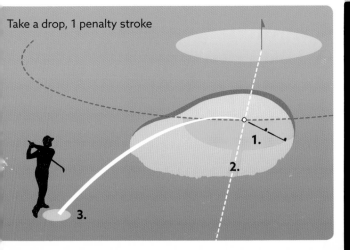

Take a drop, 1 penalty stroke

1.

2.

3.

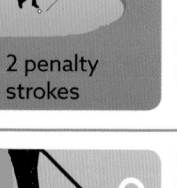

Wrong ball (R15)

If you have played the wrong ball, this stroke does not count but you will incur 2 penalty strokes. You have to go back and play the correct ball (put the wrong ball back and recreate its original lie).

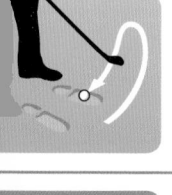

Ball rolls into your own footprints (R13)

If your ball rolls back into your own prints in the sand, there is nothing you can do about it. You have to play the ball as it lies unless you declare it unplayable (with 1 penalty stroke, see previous page).

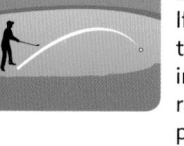

Ball stays in bunker (R13)

If you have not managed to get the ball out of the bunker and it is therefore now lying further in front of the *same* bunker, you are allowed to rake the marks of your first shot before you play your next shot but you are still not permitted to ground the club in the sand.

Ball hit out of bounds/ lost ball (R13/27)

If you have hit your ball from the bunker out of bounds or to a place where you cannot find it, you have to drop a ball on the spot where the last stroke was played from, with 1 penalty stroke—back into the bunker in this case. However, you are allowed to rake the sand *before* dropping the ball.

Striking the ball more than once (R14)

If you strike the ball more than once when playing a shot, you have to add 1 penalty stroke to it.

Margin (Def.)

A ball is in a water hazard as soon as it touches its margin. The stakes themselves are within the water hazard, i.e. the margin runs along the outside of them.

Ball only thought to be in the water hazard (R26/27)

If a ball has headed *in the direction* of a water hazard, but you cannot see exactly where it comes to rest, you can only apply the water hazard rule if it is virtually certain that the ball is in the hazard. Otherwise, it has to be treated as an ordinary "lost ball"—take a drop on the site of the last stroke (tee up on the teeing ground), 1 penalty stroke.

Do not ground your club

Ball in the water hazard—options (R13/26)

If your ball is in a water hazard, you basically have two options.

1. Without penalty, play the ball as it lies* (there are, however, some special factors to be taken into account).
2. With 1 penalty stroke, take a drop outside the water hazard (water hazard rule).

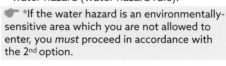

☞ *If the water hazard is an environmentally-sensitive area which you are not allowed to enter, you *must* proceed in accordance with the 2nd option.

Water hazard

Water hazard rule [R26]

If your ball is lying in a water hazard or is lost in one, you are permitted to drop outside the hazard as follows.

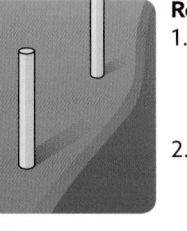

Regular water hazard (yellow)

1. Take a drop on the backwards extension of the line from the hole to the entry point (point X where the ball last crossed the margin of the hazard), 1 penalty stroke.
2. Take a drop on the site of the last stroke (tee up on the teeing ground), 1 penalty stroke.

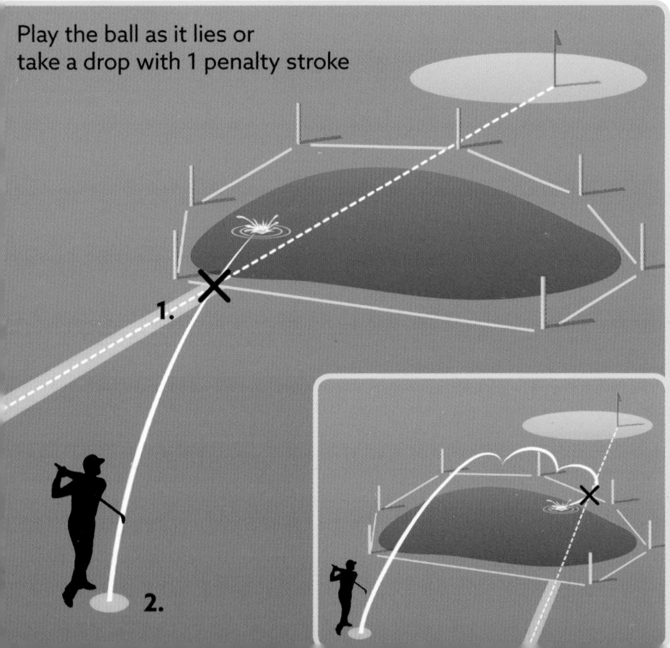

Play the ball as it lies or
take a drop with 1 penalty stroke

1.

2.

Lateral water hazard (red)

The same options (1.+2.) as with regular water hazards (yellow) *plus*

3. Take a drop within 2 club-lengths of the entry point (X), 1 penalty stroke.
4. Take a drop within 2 club-lengths of the point opposite the entry point (spot on the opposite side of the lateral water hazard at the same distance from the hole), 1 penalty stroke.

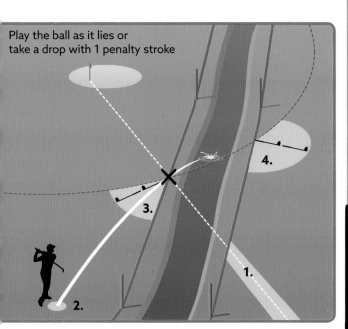

Play the ball as it lies or
take a drop with 1 penalty stroke

4.

Wate
Haza

3.

1.

2.

☛ Bear the Local Rules in mind—it is possible that a so-called dropping zone has been provided for as an *additional* option.

Identifying the ball ^(R12)

If you cannot tell whether the ball found is yours, you are allowed to mark it and pick it up for identification. However, before doing so, you must inform a fellow-player of this and give him the opportunity to observe the procedure; otherwise, you will incur 1 penalty stroke. If necessary, you may clean the ball but only to the extent needed for identification. The ball is then to be put back on exactly the same spot.

Do not touch the ground/ water ^(R13)

You are not allowed to test the condition of the water hazard before playing a stroke, i.e. do not touch the ground or the water with your hand or when making a practice swing and do not ground your club (however you are permitted to touch high grass); otherwise, you will incur 2 penalty strokes. You are allowed to put clubs down in a water hazard.

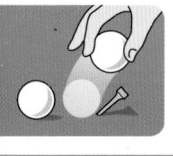

Balls close to each other ^(R22)

If two balls are so close together that they obstruct each other, one ball can be marked, picked up and put back again after the other one has been played.

Advice and line of play ^(R8)

You are allowed to ask about distances as well as the position of hazards or out of bounds margins. If you cannot see the flag you are allowed to ask someone to indicate the line of play. However, questions or advice on the choice of club or how to play a shot would incur 2 penalty

Loose impediments (R23)

Twigs, leaves, stones or other *natural* objects *cannot* be touched or removed before playing a stroke in a water hazard—2 penalty strokes in the event of a breach.

Movable obstructions (R24)

Signs, stakes (yellow, red) or other *artificial* objects can be removed without penalty. If the ground or water is touched in doing so no penalty is incurred. If the ball moves as a result, put it back without penalty.

Immovable obstructions (R24)

If your ball is lying in a water hazard relief is *not* given from bridges, pipes and other fixed, artificial objects. However, if you play the ball as it lies, you are allowed to touch the obstruction with the club (e.g. grounding the club on a bridge).

Abnormal ground conditions (R25)

Puddles, animal tracks, etc. do *not* entitle the player to relief in a water hazard. The ball has to be played as it lies, or it can be dropped under penalty of 1 stroke in accordance with the water hazard rule (see above).

Unplayable lie (R28)

In a water hazard, you *cannot* declare your ball unplayable—proceed in accordance with the water hazard rule (see above).

Water hazar

Ball played from a water hazard
... and the wrong ball hit (R15)

If you have played a stroke in a water hazard but have hit the wrong ball the stroke does not count. You will incur 2 penalty strokes and you have to go back and play the correct ball (put the wrong ball back).

2 penalty strokes

Ball played from a water hazard
... and hit into the water (R26)

If you have played a stroke in a water hazard but have not managed to hit the ball out, the stroke will of course count, but you are still entitled to proceed in accordance with the *water hazard rule* (with 1 penalty stroke, see above). The site of the last stroke is then not only the appropriate spot *in* the water hazard but also the site where you played your last stroke *outside* of the hazard.

Ball played from a water hazard
... and hit out of bounds or lost (R26)

If you have hit your ball out of the water hazard and have lost it or hit it out of bounds, you have to drop a ball, with 1 penalty stroke, on the site of the last stroke—back into the water hazard in this case. However, you could also accept another 1-stroke penalty and proceed in accordance with the *water hazard rule* (see above).

Striking the ball more than once (R14)

If you strike the ball more than once when playing a shot, you have to add 1 penalty stroke to it.

Margin (Def.)

A ball is out of bounds when the *entire ball* lies out of bounds. The out of bounds posts (white) are themselves out of bounds, i.e. the margin runs along the course side of the posts. The best way to determine whether a ball is out of bounds is by standing behind a post and bringing it in line with the next post.

☞ Watch out for out of bounds which are specified in the *Local Rules* but which may not be marked in white.

Ball out of bounds (R27)

If your ball is lying out of bounds, you only have one option—to take a drop on the site of the last stroke (tee up on the teeing ground), 1 penalty stroke.

However, if you have already played a provisional ball this now becomes the ball in play with 1 penalty stroke.

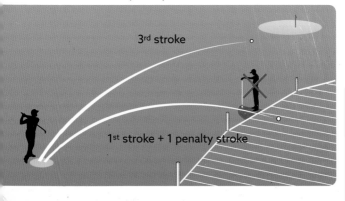

3rd stroke

1st stroke + 1 penalty stroke

Out/
prov.
ball

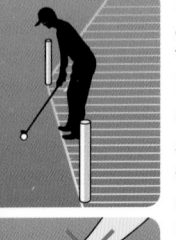

Player out of bounds but ball on the course ^(Def./R13/23/24/25)

You are allowed to stand out of bounds to play a ball which is not out of bounds. In doing so, you can remove *loose impediments* (natural) and *movable obstructions* (artificial) which are lying out of bounds, without penalty. However, you are *not* given free relief from *immovable obstructions* and *abnormal ground conditions* (puddles, ground under repair, animal tracks) which are out of bounds.

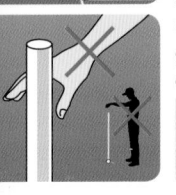

👉 You are *never* given relief from objects which mark out of bounds, whether they are movable or not.

Playing a provisional ball ^(R27)

If you suspect that you will not be able to find your ball or that it has come to rest out of bounds, you should play a provisional ball to save time. Announce that this is "provisional" and take a drop on the site of the last stroke (tee up on the teeing ground). Then, play this ball until you reach the approximate position where you believe the original ball to be.

Play a provisional ball

You can only play a provisional ball *before* you go forward to look for your first ball. However, you are permitted to go forward for up to approximately 50 yards/ 45 meters. If you have already searched further away and then go back to play a would-be provisional ball, it is actually *not* a provisional ball but a new ball in play (with 1 penalty stroke).

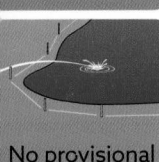

No provisional ball

👉 If your ball has landed in a *water hazard*, you do *not* have the option of playing a provisional ball.

Provisional ball not announced (R27)

If you play a second ball and do not explicitly announce that it is "provisional", it becomes the new ball in play under penalty of 1 stroke. In this case, the original ball is "lost" and can no longer be played under any circumstances (this would be playing the wrong ball).

Provisional ball in an excellent position (R27)

If you hit a wonderful shot with your provisional ball, it could be to your advantage not to find the original ball at all. In this case, you can simply not search for the first ball. However, you *cannot pronounce* the first ball "lost" *by declaration*. If you do find the original ball (within 5 minutes and it is not out of bounds), you *have* to continue play with it.

Provisional ball hit from a spot nearer to the hole than where the original ball is believed to be (R27)

You are allowed to play your provisional ball until you reach the approximate position where you believe your original ball to be. Your provisional ball is allowed to go past this position; however, you are not allowed to play a stroke with the provisional ball past this point. If you have played a shot such as this before finding the original ball, the provisional ball automatically becomes the new ball in play with 1 penalty stroke.

Out/
prov.
ball

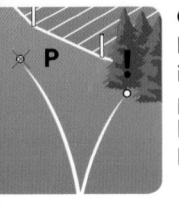

Original ball found—on the course (R27)

If you find your original ball within 5 minutes and it is not out of bounds, you *have* to continue to play with it. You *have* to pick up the provisional ball and the strokes made with the provisional ball do not count.

Original ball found—but unplayable (R27/28)

If you find your original ball (within 5 minutes and it is not out of bounds), you *have* to continue to play with it—even if it has a poor or unplayable lie. The provisional ball is not to be played under any circumstances (that would be playing the wrong ball).

If you declare the original ball unplayable, you must proceed in strict accordance with the unplayable ball rule and maybe even return to the site of the last stroke once again.

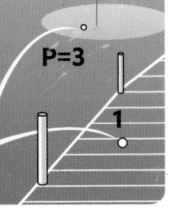

Original ball out of bounds or cannot be found (R27)

If your original ball is out of bounds or if you have not found it within 5 minutes, the provisional ball becomes the ball in play with 1 penalty stroke, i.e. all the strokes played with both the original ball and with the provisional ball count, plus 1 penalty stroke.

Green and fringe (Def.)
The ball is on the green if it touches the green. According to the rules, the fringe is not part of the green but is classed as through the green (see "Fairway & rough").

Order of play (R10)
It is always the turn of the player whose ball is furthest away from the hole (regardless of whether, for example, one ball is on the green and another is still off it). Nevertheless, this is often deviated from on and around the green to *save time*. No penalty is then incurred. However, if the players have *agreed* upon the wrong order for *tactical* reasons, they will be punished with disqualification.

MATCH PLAY: If a player makes a stroke when it was not his turn he will not incur a penalty, however the opponent may immediately require the player to cancel his stroke and replay it in the correct order.

Marking and picking up the ball (R16/20)
On the green, you are permitted to mark the ball's position and then pick it up and clean it. The ball should be marked with a ball-marker or a coin. Marking the ball with a tee, a pitch repairer, etc. is permitted but not advisable.

Ball moved when marking it (R18/20)
If the ball or the marker is moved accidentally when marking, picking up or replacing the ball, put it back without penalty.

Green

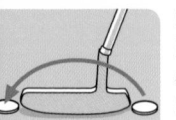

Marking to the side [(R20)]

If your ball-marker is on the line of putt of another player, it should be marked to the side (move it by one or two putter head lengths).

☞ It is important to remember to return the marker to its original position afterwards. If it is not put back and the ball is played, the stroke counts but you will incur 2 penalty strokes for playing from the wrong spot.

Note: If a ball is deflected by a ball-marker, this is classed as the "rub of the green"—play the ball as it lies without penalty.

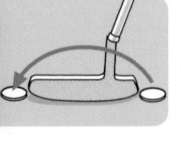

Ball marked by another person [(R20)]

You are allowed to ask another player to mark your ball. Either the person who picked it up or the player himself must put the ball back.

Wrong ball [(R15)]

If you realize that the ball you are playing is not your ball, you have to go back and play the correct ball. The strokes made with the wrong ball do not count but you will incur 2 penalty strokes. If you cannot find the correct ball, you have to return to the place where you last played the correct ball from and drop another ball with 1 additional penalty stroke (tee up on the teeing ground).

☞ If you hole out with the wrong ball and do not rectify your mistake, you will be *disqualified*.

Embedded ball (R16)

If your ball has become embedded in the green, mark its position, pick it up and repair the pitch-mark. Then, put the ball back without penalty.

Damaged ball (R5)

If your ball has become dented, deformed, or damaged significantly in any way (not just scratched) during play of a hole, you can replace it without penalty. However, before doing so, you must inform a fellow-player and give him the opportunity to examine the ball. Otherwise, you will incur 1 penalty stroke.

☞ Note: This procedure is allowed on the entire course; however, in practice, it is mainly used on the green.

Ball moved when addressing it or during a practice swing (R18)

If you move your ball when addressing it or as a result of a careless practice swing (does not count as a stroke), you must put it back and you will incur 1 penalty stroke.

Advice and line of putt (R8/14)

You are not permitted to ask for or give advice, e.g. concerning the line of putt ("Does the green break from left to right?", "Watch out, it has a bigger break than you think."); otherwise 2 penalty strokes will be incurred. A player who is given unsolicited advice does not receive any penalty strokes. You are not allowed to ask anyone to stand on the extension of the line of putt while playing a stroke.

Green

Do not test the green (R16)

You are not allowed to test the green by rolling a ball or by roughening the surface of the green (2 penalty strokes).

Do not improve the line of putt (R16)

You are not allowed to improve the line of putt by treading on it or touching it (2 penalty strokes). The only action which is permitted is to repair pitch-marks and old hole plugs on the line of putt. Spike marks in particular are to be left as they are but should be repaired on completion of the hole.

Repairing pitch-marks —no penalty

Loose impediments (R23)

Leaves, twigs, stones or other *natural* objects can be removed without penalty. On the green, you are also permitted to remove sand and loose soil (but not on the fringe or anywhere else). However, in doing so, uneven areas on the line of putt are not to be smoothed out. If the ball or marker moves as a result, put it back without penalty.

Movable obstructions (R24)

Lost gloves, score cards and other artificial objects can be removed without penalty. If the ball moves as a result, put it back without penalty.

Sprinklers (R24)

Sprinklers are usually positioned off the green but may be near or on the fringe. This part of the course is deemed "through the green" and therefore the player is only given free relief if the sprinkler interferes with his *stance* or *swing*. If the sprinkler is merely on the *line of play* the ball has to be played as it lies.

If the ball is on the *green* and the sprinkler is on the *line of putt*—place the ball at the nearest point where the interference no longer occurs, but not nearer to the hole, without penalty. (Note: This point could be off the green.)

Puddles and other abnormal ground conditions (R25)

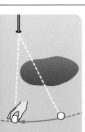

You are entitled to relief if your ball is lying within such an area, if you would have to take your stance within it or, additionally, if such an area is on your line of putt. *Place* the ball at the nearest point where the interference no longer occurs, not nearer to the hole, without penalty. (Note: This point could be off the green.)

Ball deflected by marker (R19)

If a ball is deflected by a ball-marker, this is classed as the "rub of the green"—play the ball as it lies without penalty.

Ball hits another ball (R19)

If you putt on the green and your ball hits a ball at rest on the green, you will incur 2 penalty strokes. You have to play your ball as it lies and the ball which was moved must be put back. (If this happens after you have played from *off* the green, you will not incur a penalty.)

MATCH PLAY: Continue play without penalty and put the moved ball back.

Green

Ball hits the flagstick or the person tending it [R17]

If you are putting on the green and your ball hits either the flagstick (irrespective of whether it is in the hole or has been taken out and put aside) or the person tending it, you will incur 2 penalty strokes. The ball has to be played as it lies.

However, if you have played from *off* the green and the ball has hit the *untended* flagstick in the hole, you will not incur a penalty.

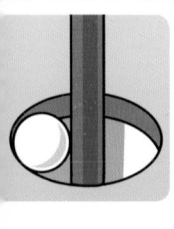

2 penalty strokes

Ball wedged on the flagstick [R17]

If your ball is wedged between the flagstick and the rim of the hole, but is still not beneath the lip, you are allowed to move the flagstick or to take it out carefully so that the ball falls into the hole. It is then classed as having been holed with the last stroke.

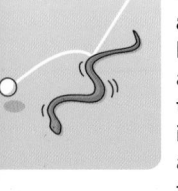

Ball hits another player or an outside agency [R19]

If, after a shot played on the green, your ball hits another player (except for the person tending the flagstick, see above), an animal (except for insects and worms), the ball of another group or any other outside agency that *moves* or *is alive*, the stroke has to be cancelled and must be replayed without penalty (place the ball).

MATCH PLAY: If your ball hits the opponent or his equipment no penalty is incurred. You can choose to continue to play the ball as it lies or you can cancel the stroke and replay it (place the ball).

Put it back, no penalty

Ball at rest moved by an outside agency (R18)

If your ball at rest is moved by an outside agency (spectator, animal, fellow-competitor, other ball, etc.) you have to put your ball back without penalty. If your ball has been picked up and taken away, you can place *another* ball on the spot where the ball was, without penalty.

MATCH PLAY: If the ball was moved by your opponent the opponent incurs 1 penalty stroke. The ball has to be put back.

10 sec.

Ball on the edge of the hole (R16)

If your ball comes to rest on the edge of the hole you must approach the hole without delay and you are allowed to wait for 10 seconds. If the ball drops in within this time, it is classed as having been holed. If it falls in after the 10 seconds are up, it is also classed as holed but you have to add 1 penalty stroke.

Ball bounces back out of the hole (Def.)

If your ball falls into the hole and bounces back out again it is not classed as having been holed as the ball has to come to rest in the hole. You have to hole the ball again by playing it as it lies.

Double green (R25)

If your ball lands on a double green in the area of the wrong hole, you have to play the ball as it lies. If the wrong hole is in your way, you are entitled to relief. Place the ball at the nearest point where the hole is no longer in the way, without penalty.

Green

Wrong green (R25)
If your ball lands on the wrong green, you are *not* allowed to play the ball. You *have* to take a free drop (see "Fairway & rough" section under the heading "Wrong green").

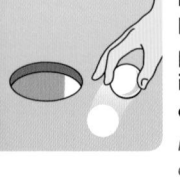

Putt conceded/ ball not holed (R2/3/18)
In stroke play, strokes *cannot* be conceded. If a player picks up his ball by mistake, he has to put it back with 1 penalty stroke and then hole it, otherwise he may be disqualified.

MATCH PLAY: The player can concede that his opponent has holed out with his next stroke. Conceded shots can neither be refused nor withdrawn. If the player who has been given the hole plays it to the end anyway the result is not affected.

Careless putting (R14)
The ball is always to be hit, not pushed or scraped (2 penalty strokes). However, you are allowed to hit it with any side of the clubhead, e.g. even with the back of the putter.

Protection from the elements (R14)
You are never allowed to accept protection offered by a *third party while* playing a stroke (2 penalty strokes).

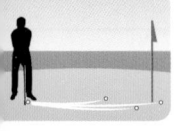

Practice putting and chipping (R7)
When you have finished the hole, you are allowed to putt or chip again for practice if this does not delay play (and if it has not been ruled out by the Conditions of Competition).

Ball at rest is moved ...

... by the player himself or his equipment (R18)

Accidentally. When looking for a ball*, addressing it or making a practice swing—put the ball back, 1 penalty stroke.

(*Exception: When looking for a ball in *abnormal ground conditions* or in *obstructions*, or for a ball which is *covered* by sand—put the ball back without penalty.)

Loose impediments. When removing *loose impediments*—put the ball back, 1 penalty stroke (exception: green—without penalty).

Movable obstructions. When removing artificial objects (e.g. the rake)—put the ball back without penalty.

Marking. When marking a ball on the green—put the ball back without penalty.

... by an outside agency (R18)

If the ball is moved by an outside agency e.g. by a fellow-player, a spectator, an animal, etc.—put the ball back without penalty.

... by another ball (R18)

If the ball is hit by another ball and is moved as a result—put the ball back without penalty (the other ball must be played as it lies).

... by the wind (Def./R13)

If the ball is moved by a gust of wind or if it moves of its own accord—play the ball as it lies from the new position without penalty.

... by the opponent in match play (R18)

When searching, no penalty, otherwise 1 penalty stroke for the opponent. The ball must be put back.

Ball moved

Ball in motion hits ...

... the player or his equipment (R19)

If the ball hits the player himself or his equipment—play the ball as it lies, 1 penalty stroke.

... an outside agency (R17/19)

If the ball hits an outside agency (fellow-player, spectator, animal, tree, electricity pole, etc.)—play the ball as it lies without penalty.

(Exception: Green—if, after a stroke on the green, the ball hits something which moves or is alive—replay the stroke without penalty.)

If the ball hits the person tending the flag—play the ball as it lies, 2 penalty strokes.

... another ball (R19)

If the ball hits another ball at rest—play the ball as it lies without penalty (exception in stroke play: Green—if both balls were on the green before the stroke was played—2 penalty strokes). The ball that was moved must be put back.

... the flagstick (R17)

If, after being played from off the green, the ball hits the *untended* flagstick in the hole— play the ball as it lies without penalty.

If, after being played on the green, the ball hits the *untended* flagstick in the hole—play the ball as it lies, 2 penalty strokes.

If the ball hits the flagstick, which is being tended or has been removed and put aside (irrespective of where the shot was made from)—play the ball as it lies, 2 penalty strokes.

... the opponent in match play (R19)

No penalty. Either continue to play the ball as it lies or cancel the stroke and replay it (take a drop, tee up on the teeing ground, place it on the green).

To supplement this quick guide we recommend

Golf Etiquette
Quick Reference
A golfer's guide to
correct conduct
ISBN 978-3-909596-77-5

Trouble Shots
and Quick Fix Guide
Golf tips for around
the course
ISBN 978-3-909596-96-6

Yves C. Ton-That is a rules official and has a law degree. He has written ten books on golf which have been translated into more than 20 languages. Some of his works are awards winners. In addition to this, he has written numerous articles for various golf magazines and advises golf clubs and associations throughout the world about rules issues. He has a handicap of 5.

Published by Artigo Publishing International
www.expertgolf.com, ISBN 978-3-909596-84-3
10th edition, 2016, © 2004-2016 Yves C. Ton-That

E✗PERT GOLF
get there

Available as a customized special edition

Message from the Board,
advertising, Local Rules etc.

Logo cover

GOLF RULES.
A PRACTICAL GUIDE FOR USE ON THE COURSE

Customized covers include the front and back of the cover page. Minimum order quantity is 250 copies. For orders and further information please contact us at books@expertgolf.com.

Overview of the relief procedures

(For the exact procedure please refer to the relevant index tab.)

	Fairway & rough	Bunker	Water hazard	Green
Loose impediments — Remove without penalty. If the ball moves:	✓ replace the ball, 1 penalty stroke	✗	✗	✓ replace the ball, no penalty
Movable obstructions — Remove without penalty. If the ball moves:	✓ replace the ball, no penalty	✓ replace the ball, no penalty	✓ replace the ball, no penalty	✓ replace the ball, no penalty
Immovable obstructions — Relief in case of interference of lie/ stance/ swing	✓	✓	✗	✓ also if line of putt is interfered with
Abnormal ground conditions — Relief in case of interference of lie/ stance/ swing	✓	✓	✗	✓ also if line of putt is interfered with
Declaring a ball unplayable (under penalty of 1 stroke) — Relief in case of interference of lie/ stance/ swing	✓	✓	✗	✓